WITH ALL DUE RESPECT

HOW *to* BIBLICALLY
RESPOND *to* AUTHORITY

LARRY CHAPPELL

First published in 2014 by Striving Together Publications, a ministry
of Lancaster Baptist Church, Lancaster, CA 93535. Striving Together
Publications is committed to providing tried, trusted, and proven
resources that will further equip local churches to carry out the
Great Commission. Your comments and suggestions are valued.

Striving Together Publications
4020 E. Lancaster Blvd.
Lancaster, CA 93535
800.201.7748
strivingtogether.com

Cover design by Andrew Jones
Layout by Craig Parker
Writing assistance by Kristina Primo
Special thanks to our proofreaders

The author and publication team have put forth every effort to give proper
credit to quotes and thoughts that are not original with the author. It is not
our intent to claim originality with any quote or thought that could not
readily be tied to an original source.

ISBN 978-1-59894-256-9
Printed in the United States of America

Contents

Don't Tell Me What To Do

Honour all men. Love the brotherhood. Fear God. Honour the king.—1 Peter 2:17

I do not like to be told what to do—at least not by airlines or flight attendants.

I don't like being told which belongings I can and cannot take with me. I don't like being told to take off my shoes and proceed through a machine that does a full body scan. But above all, I don't like being told to turn off my cell phone for take off. Pretty silly, right?

Except, it doesn't seem silly to me in the moment when the flight attendant begins going from row to row telling everyone to turn off every electronic device. Even as I begin to comply, I suddenly remember people I need to text, emails I need to answer, and social media updates I want to check.

Somehow the flight attendant knows my phone is still on because no matter how innocent I look or how carefully I avoid eye contact, she always comes by again telling me to turn off my phone. And when she does, the same thoughts come to mind: *My being on my phone is not going to change anyone's life. I have kept my phone on a number of times and we haven't crashed yet.*

By nature, we are born rebels. Even the most soft spoken among us know how to push back, how to quietly rebel.

What makes matters worse is that we are living in a rebellious society. A society that encourages, even enables, rebellion.

Teenagers probably defy authority more than any other age group—at least rebellion is most easy to spot in teenagers. Teachers are mocked. Parents are questioned. Reasons are demanded. Instructions are ignored. Ironically, no other group demands more respect than teenagers do, yet they so often give none.

For years, modern culture has been telling teenagers to question authority. And the fruit of that questioning? Well, society has never been in more trouble than it is in today.

As Christians, we know that we are to reject worldly philosophy and live in a way that is aligned with God's Word. But what exactly does that look like in relation to how we interact with authorities?

For starters, it means we obey flight attendants— no matter how annoyed we may be with their rules! More seriously, it means we seek out what God has to say about authority, and we determine to submit to God's commands.

The Bible has much to say about the establishment of authority, the attack on authority, and the response that Christians should have towards authority. These are the truths which I would like to explore with you in these pages.

Perhaps you have strained relationships with one or more authority figures in your life. I pray you will apply these truths from God's Word and, to the best of your ability, strengthen those relationships.

Perhaps you're doing great and already have healthy relationships with those in authority. I pray these truths will encourage you to maintain these relationships.

Perhaps you have mixed relationships with authority—some great and some not so great.

In any case, I pray you will approach these truths from God's Word with an open mind and a yielded heart. We may not think the flight attendant has the right to tell us what to do, but God most certainly does! Let's see what He says…

CHAPTER ONE

Says Who?

God's Establishment of Authority

Let every soul be subject unto the higher powers. For there is no power but of God: the powers that be are ordained of God. Whosoever therefore resisteth the power, resisteth the ordinance of God: and they that resist shall receive to themselves damnation. For rulers are not a terror to good works, but to the evil. Wilt thou then not be afraid of the power? do that which is good, and thou shalt have praise of the same: For he is the minister of God to thee for good. But if thou do that

which is evil, be afraid; for he beareth not the
sword in vain: for he is the minister of God,
a revenger to execute wrath upon him that
doeth evil. Wherefore ye must needs be subject,
not only for wrath, but also for conscience sake.
For for this cause pay ye tribute also: for they
are God's ministers, attending continually
upon this very thing. Render therefore to all
their dues: tribute to whom tribute is due;
custom to whom custom; fear to whom fear;
honour to whom honour.—ROMANS 13:1–7

The idea of questioning authority is really nothing new.

The Apostle Paul penned the verses above at a time when Rome was the superpower of the world. Christians were persecuted, and it was only going to get worse. Understanding these difficulties, Paul gave instruction to suffering believers to teach them how to relate and respond to the government.

Civil government is one of three institutions ordained by God. The other two are the family and the local church. Although Romans 13 is written in context of governmental authority, the principles in this passage are applicable in every context of authority.

In this chapter, let's look at seven universal laws of authority. These are as relevant today as they were in the first century, and they are as applicable to your life as they were to persecuted Christians two millennia ago.

Universal Law #1: Everybody Answers to Somebody

"Let every soul be subject unto the higher powers."

No one escapes the principle of authority. And, as we'll see in our next chapter, this is to your benefit.

Many young people do everything within their power to avoid being told what to do. Some teenagers struggle throughout high school to break from their authority. They somehow think that as they walk across the platform and receive their diplomas something magical will happen, and they will never have to answer to authority again.

False.

Everyone answers to somebody. Every church member has a pastor. Every employee has a boss. Every citizen has the law. Every man has God. No one will ever get to a place where he will not answer to someone. In fact, those who attempt to escape authority to gain freedom often find that the result is greater restraint.

For example, David Glasheen was a former Wall Street investor. In the 1980s, he made some bad trades and within days lost tens of millions of dollars of his own money and money that other people had entrusted to him.

Disheartened and determined to get away from all authority, Glasheen took his remaining wealth and bought an island. He bought this island for himself and his dog, expecting to never have to deal with another person for the rest of his life.

For almost twenty-five years, Glasheen was the king of his own island, building sandcastles and drinking coconut juice sunset after sunset. Then one day, someone going through paperwork concerning the purchase of the island discovered a discrepancy that voided the purchase of the island. Shortly after, Glasheen was served an eviction notice from his own island. Bummer!

If you have a strained relationship with your authority—whether it be your parents or a teacher or your youth pastor—don't make the mistake of thinking that by avoiding that authority your problems will simply disappear. They won't. You will deal with authority for the rest of your life, and your responses will decide whether you live in misery or not.

Now is the time to recognize this truth and decide to respect and learn from your authorities. As we'll see later, this is a choice you will be glad you made!

Universal Law #2: Authority Is Established and Sustained by God

"For there is no power but of God: the powers that be are ordained of God."

When I was in college, I worked at a law firm. One of the phrases we regularly used in legal papers was "the powers that be." In plain English, that phrase simply refers to whoever happens to be in charge at the time.

That phrase is also used in Romans 13: *"The powers that be are ordained of God."* So every person in authority—whoever happens to be in charge in your life—has been allowed by God to be in that position of authority. This is true whether the person is the ruler of a country, a youth pastor, or a parent. God created the principle of authority, and He sustains that authority according to His perfect will.

Think for a moment about the authorities in your life—maybe your parents, a coach, or a school teacher. God has ordained them and sustained them. This does not mean that they are perfect (as you well know, they are not). But it does mean that God has allowed them to be in your life despite their imperfections.

I don't always understand why God allows certain men to be in authority. I think of Kim Jong-un in North Korea who represses his own people and always seems to be threatening to drop nuclear bombs to wipe out America. I think of Adolf Hitler who was responsible for the deaths of millions of people. I can't explain why God allows people like that to be in authority, but He does. Proverbs 21:1 says, *"The king's heart is in the hand of the* LORD, *as the rivers of water: he turneth it whithersoever he will."*

Our God is infinite and all-knowing. We can't even begin to fathom all that He does, but we can know that He works all things together for good to them that love Him: *"And we know that all things work together for good to them that love God, to them who are the called according to his purpose"* (Romans 8:28).

God gives us His promise that He will take even the bad, the imperfect, the frustrating aspects of our lives—which may include certain authorities—and make it all work together for our good. But we must be willing to obey His commands even when we don't understand.

I know the authorities in your life are not all perfect. (Yes, I speak from experience!) They will let you down. They will make bad judgment calls. But you must realize that God has allowed them to be in your life for a reason, and you have a biblical

command to obey, respect, and honor their authority.
(This does not mean that you obey if they tell you to
do something sinful or that you do not report them to
government authority if they cross a line by engaging
in crime or violating your body. Abuse is different
than imperfection or a mistake.)

When an authority figure in your life does make
a mistake, remember that God knows and that He will
work it out for good. You are not responsible for their
actions, but you will be held accountable for your
reaction. Choose now to honor authority and claim
the promises of God.

Universal Law #3: How We Respond to Authority Is a Reflection of How We Respond to God

*"Whosoever therefore resisteth the power, resisteth the
ordinance of God:"*

To rebel against any authority God has placed in
your life is not only to rebel against them but to rebel
against God.

This reminds me of my school days when we would get a substitute teacher. (This was always either a very bad thing or a very good thing.) Before the substitute would come in, we would get a lecture from our teacher about obeying the substitute and helping him if he needed anything. We were told to respect the substitute. And when we mistreated the substitute, we not only disrespected him, but we were disrespecting our teacher who had established that authority in his absence.

Similarly, how you and I respond to authority is a reflection of how we respond to God. The authority is like a substitute teacher. When we resist their authority, we actually resist God's authority.

You cannot be right with God and wrong with the authority in your life. You cannot pick and choose which authority to obey and which to disregard.

Admittedly, some authorities are easier to obey than others. Those who are constantly affirming us and who we easily see have our best interest at heart are easy for us to respond favorably towards.

Those who do not require much of us are also easy to appreciate.

Understand, however, that responding rightly to all authorities is a sign of maturity—an expression of your submission to God Himself.

If your youth pastor asks you to run around the church building fifty-two times and you willingly obey, but you refuse to take out the trash when your parent asks you to, you demonstrate (among other things) an immaturity in your understanding of authority. You cannot be selective in your appreciation and respect for authority and still be living in accordance with God's universal laws of authority.

The Bible does not say, "Let every soul be subject unto the higher powers that he likes." It does not say, "Let every soul be subject unto the higher powers that deserve respect." It says, *"Let every soul be subject unto the higher powers."* Period. (Just in case you didn't see it there.)

Universal Law #4: Rejecting Authority Makes Us Vulnerable and Weak

"...and they that resist shall receive to themselves damnation."

I cannot emphasize enough that authority is there for your protection. When the authorities in your life set boundaries, it is not because they want to trap you and keep you from enjoying life. They are trying to protect you from the potential danger that they know lies outside those boundaries.

Let's think of it this way: Have you ever had the opportunity to watch Shark Week? I love Shark Week! (Cue the music from *Jaws*.) My favorite times of the year are as follows: 1. Christmas, 2. my birthday, and 3. Shark Week! (Oops...forgot my anniversary.)

Shark Week provides an opportunity to get as close as I'd ever want to be to a great white shark. But let's just say, hypothetically of course, that I lost my mind and wanted to get in the water with a school of aggressive sharks. I can guarantee you that the only way I would ever jump in is if I had a shark cage. Not just any shark cage—the biggest, most protective shark cage ever known to man! I'm pretty sure you feel the same way.

In fact, let's say that you also lose your mind and want to swim with sharks. Like me, you start in a strong, protective shark cage. But suppose after swimming with the sharks in your protected cage, you decide that you want to get a little closer to the sharks. You decide that you no longer want the restrictions of the cage. You even argue that none of your other friends have shark cages, so you don't need one either.

You do realize, however, that you should probably retain some sort of protection, so you decide to remove just one of the bars on your shark cage. It's just one bar. But you are now more vulnerable than before. One isn't enough, so you pull out another. If you continue to remove those bars to get a "better view," you know what will eventually happen—you will become shark supper!

The shark cage represents the authority in your life as a whole. It is designed to protect you. Those bars that keep you from being vulnerable are the individuals that God has placed in your life—your parents, pastor, youth pastor, teachers, boss, etc. Choosing to remove any one of them, to rebel against them, is to make yourself susceptible to spiritual attack.

First Peter 5:8 cautions, *"Be sober, be vigilant; because your adversary the devil, as a roaring lion, walketh about, seeking whom he may devour."* Reject the authorities in your life, and you make yourself vulnerable to become lion lunch!

This rebellion that removes safety comes in two forms. Active rebellion is easy to identify. It is found in the young person who blatantly goes against every principle found in God's Word and disrespects authority openly.

Passive rebellion, however, is harder to spot. This is found in the young person who won't openly go against authority, but will talk about them when they are not around. He knows how to play the part when authority is around, but when that authority is gone, the true character of that young person is revealed. Either way, the result is still the same. Rebellion corrodes the protective boundaries of authority in your life.

Proverbs 11:14 says, *"Where no counsel is, the people fall: but in the multitude of counsellors there is safety."* When your pastor preaches a biblical principle and you choose to reject that principle, when your teacher advises you to make wise choices and you decide that your way is better, when your parents set boundaries and you decide to cross those lines, you make yourself weak. When you rebel against them, you remove yourself from safety.

If you live a life that is continually "crossing the line," you will eventually discover the danger from which your authorities have tried to protect you. *"But every man that is tempted, when he is drawn away of his own lust, and enticed. Then when lust hath conceived, it bringeth forth sin: and sin, when it is finished, bringeth forth death"* (James 1:14–15).

Universal Law #5: A Poor Relationship with Authority Distorts Reality

"For rulers are not a terror to good works, but to the evil."

Some young people have the idea that all authority is out to get them. The reality is that becoming comfortable with sin makes you uncomfortable with authority. If you have done nothing wrong, you have nothing to hide from authority.

A few years ago, my wife and I were in a car accident. The car was totaled, so we called my mom to see if she could come pick us up. As we were moving things from our trunk into her trunk, a police officer showed up. I figured he had come to fill out a traffic report. I had nothing to hide, but when he came up to talk to me, he wasn't very kind.

I had expected the officer to be a bit more consoling, considering I had just totaled my car. Instead he asked me to step aside with him so he could ask me a few questions. Then, in a serious tone, he asked, "Is there something about this accident that you aren't telling us?"

Possibilities raced through my mind, but I couldn't think of anything to tell him. It had happened just as I had said. I wanted him to tell me what I did wrong so that I could admit to it. I had a clear conscience with that authority, so I wasn't afraid of him.

Then he asked me to walk over to his car with him. When he put handcuffs on me and put me in the backseat of his car, that's when I got a bit more concerned. I still knew I hadn't broken the law, but I was wondering how long it would take him to figure that out. I didn't want my situation to become a special news report fifty years from now: "Baptist youth pastor wrongfully accused. Sentenced to death. Narrowly escapes."

As it turns out, there had been a hit and run in the Wal-Mart parking lot a few blocks away, and the vehicle description matched our car. Same model, same color, same last three digits on the license plate.

The police thought that we had hit an elderly lady in the parking lot and had fled the scene!

I sat handcuffed in the back seat of the police car for a while. They looked at the security footage and realized that it wasn't actually us and let us go. During that time, however, I had nothing to fear (except a false accusation) because I knew I had not done anything wrong.

If you have a stressed relationship with any authority in your life, work on that relationship. Identify what is causing the strain. If it is because of sin in your life, make that right with God and with the person in authority so that your relationship with that person will be right. If you don't, your relationship with all authority—including God—will become more strained. The tighter the strain the more your perception will be distorted. You will begin to believe all authority is bad and all authority is out to get you.

Remember, there is nothing to fear from authority when you are submitting to authority and living in obedience to God.

Universal Law #6: A Healthy Relationship with Authority Creates Opportunities and Brings Joy

"Wilt thou then not be afraid of the power? do that which is good, and thou shalt have praise of the same:"

The authorities in your life carry a weighty biblical responsibility to teach you God's Word and to watch for your soul. Hebrews 13:17 says, *"Obey them that have the rule over you, and submit yourselves: for they watch for your souls, as they that must give account, that they may do it with joy, and not with grief: for that is unprofitable for you."*

Teenagers often want to be in charge, believing that it will get them out from under authority. They want to tell others what to do rather than being told what to do. The truth is that everyone in authority will one day give account for what they have done with the authority God has given them.

When you submit to authority, when you are right with them and they are right with God, everyone is happy! Your parents are happy, your teachers are happy, your pastor is happy, you are happy. Submission brings joy!

An unhealthy relationship with authority can create burdens for you even years down the road. When I first started working in youth ministry, I was asked to take a teenage guy out to lunch. He was as rebellious as a teenager could be, even in a one-on-one situation. Although I was buying this guy lunch and trying to be a blessing to him, he was being as disrespectful as he could be. Years later, I received a job reference request from this guy's prospective employer. I was surprised, but I filled it out honestly. If the employer read my reference, I doubt the guy got the job.

Just as rebellion and disobedience have negative consequences, submission and obedience result in favor and blessing.

The *Christian Herald* once told of a Persian legend. The story was of a certain king who needed a servant who would be obedient and faithful. Two men were candidates for the office, so he hired both at fixed wages. His first order to both of them was to pour buckets of water from a neighboring well into baskets. He told them he would come in the evening to check their work.

After pouring in one or two bucketfuls, one man said to the other, "What is the good of doing this useless work? As soon as we put the water in, it runs out of the basket."

"But we have our wages, haven't we?" the other answered. "The use is the master's business, not ours."

"I am not going to do such fool's work," replied the other. Throwing down his basket, the frustrated servant went away.

The other man continued until he had exhausted the well. Looking down into it, he saw something shining—a diamond ring. "Now I see the use of pouring the water into a basket!" he cried. "If the bucket had brought up the ring before the well was emptied, it would have been found in the basket. Our work was not useless."

The faithful servant was blessed for his obedience. When you obey the authority in your life, you too will experience blessing, not only from your authority, but also from God. If you choose a life of obedience and submission, you choose a life of true joy.

Universal Law #7: The Greatest Motivation for Obedience Should Be Your Love for God

"Wherefore ye must needs be subject, not only for wrath, but also for conscience sake."

Many young people like to obey simply to get their back patted. They want their authority to tell them "Good job" and hand them a cookie for obeying. Pretty immature when you think of it, isn't it?

If reward from your authority is your motivation, there will come a day when even a cookie won't get you to obey. Perhaps your authority will ask you to do something that you don't want to do, or you come under authority whom you don't particularly like. Then you will have returned to the point at which you rebel against God because you rebel against the authority He has given.

There are other short-sighted motives for obedience. Some young people obey because they are afraid of getting caught in disobedience. Others realize that life is much easier when they do what they are supposed to do, so they obey to avoid trouble. Others live in a continual state of fear because they know they have already done something wrong. This is a miserable way to live!

In 1811, James Madison established something called the "Conscience Fund." He had received five dollars from someone who had defrauded the government. Not really knowing what to do with the money, he established this fund. To this day, the treasury maintains the fund for anyone who wants to soothe his conscience. Since the fund was established, more than $6.5 million has been put into this fund. Most of the "donors" remain anonymous; however, letters are often included with admittance to some offense, however small, against the government. These people know that what they've done isn't right, and they need a way to clear their consciences.

It is often said that there is no softer pillow than a clear conscience. In Acts 24:16 Paul wrote, *"And herein do I exercise myself, to have always a conscience void of offense toward God, and toward men."* This is the better way. Keep your conscience clear—not out of fear or for the praise of man, but because you love God.

We will discuss this more in Chapter 3, but ultimately your love for God should be your chief motivation for obeying authority. You must decide that because you love God and you know that He has placed the authority in your life for a reason, you are going to obey that authority. You must choose to embrace the authority figures in your life, understanding that they are there for your protection. This is the happiest, most peaceful way to live!

CHAPTER TWO

Beware the Opposition

Satan's Attack Against Authority

Now the serpent was more subtil than any beast of the field which the Lord God had made. And he said unto the woman, Yea, hath God said, Ye shall not eat of every tree of the garden? And the woman said unto the serpent, We may eat of the fruit of the trees of the garden: But of the fruit of the tree which is in the midst of the garden, God hath said, Ye shall not eat of it, neither shall ye touch it, lest ye die. And the serpent said unto the woman, Ye shall not surely die: For God doth know that

*in the day ye eat thereof, then your eyes shall
be opened, and ye shall be as gods, knowing
good and evil.*—GENESIS 3:1–5

Written on every page of history is the attack on
authority. In fact, we can trace it back to the beginning
of history in the Garden of Eden.

The first attack against God's authority is
recorded in Genesis 3. God created Adam and Eve
and placed them where they had everything they
could ever need. But there was one who opposed
God and desired to bring out the worst in men. In
Revelation 12:10, he is called the *"accuser of the
brethren."* In 1 Peter 5:8 he is called *"your adversary"*
and *"a roaring lion…seeking whom he may devour."*
Satan still opposes God and seeks to turn men away
from Him.

Here's the good news. Satan still uses the same
mode of operation that he has used since Genesis 3.
Learn to recognize his wily tricks, which we will
explore in this chapter, and you can save yourself
much heartache.

So how does Satan attack authority? He uses rebellion, and he has specific ways he does it.

Rebellion Begins Subtly.

"Now the serpent was more subtil than any beast of the field which the LORD God had made."

No one wakes up one day and says, "Today, I'm going to start going against everyone who tells me to do anything!"

Rebellion never starts so obviously. It begins in the heart, and it begins with pride.

Even as God is the source of all authority, Satan is the source of all rebellion. His own rebellion against God began with pride. Isaiah 14:12–14 records the sordid story:

How art thou fallen from heaven, O Lucifer, son of the morning! how art thou cut down to the ground, which didst weaken the nations! For thou hast said in thine heart, I will ascend into heaven, I will exalt my throne above the stars of God: I will sit also upon the mount of

*the congregation, in the sides of the north: I
will ascend above the heights of the clouds; I
will be like the most High.*

Did you see where it began? Notice the phrase
"*...thou hast said in thine heart....*" Satan's own
rebellion began in his heart. Clearly, his heart was
filled with pride. Satan's pride will inevitably end in
destruction, but for now, he seeks to bring men down
with him.

In the Garden of Eden, Satan knew that he could
not blatantly ask Adam and Eve to rebel against God.
Thus, he began to sow the seeds of rebellion in their
hearts and minds. He disguised himself as a serpent.
The Bible calls this creature *subtil*, which means
"shrewd or clever."

As Christians, we are called out of a life of
disobedience to God. Ephesians 2:2 says, "*Wherein in
time past ye walked according to the course of this world,
according to the prince of the power of the air, the spirit
that now worketh in the children of disobedience.*" In
Ephesians 5:8, we read that we are no longer children

of darkness but rather children of light. Then in verse 15, God gives us an admonition: *"See then that ye walk circumspectly, not as fools, but as wise."* That word *circumspectly* simply means "cautiously." It's the idea of looking to the left, to the right, forward, and behind to prevent or avoid trouble. We are constantly to be looking around us because we have a crafty and cunning enemy who seeks to bring us down. His traps are hidden and his tricks are subtle. You must stay on guard!

In addition to the direct temptations of the devil, we have the fleshly desires of our own hearts that pull us toward rebellion. Jeremiah 17:9 warns, *"The heart is deceitful above all things, and desperately wicked: who can know it?"* When we just "follow our heart," we are likely to be pulled into sin. James 1:14 says, *"...every man is tempted, when he is drawn away of his own lust, and enticed."*

Because rebellion begins in the heart and because it begins so subtly, we must guard our hearts! *"Keep thy heart with all diligence; for out of it are the issues of life"* (Proverbs 4:23).

If the rebellion that begins in our hearts is not corrected, it will lead to action.

Rebellion Questions God's Authority.

"And he said unto the woman, Yea, hath God said, Ye shall not eat of every tree of the garden?"

Let me ask you a question: Is it ever okay to question God?

I remember the first time I was asked this question. I thought it was a trap. I remember thinking that questioning God seemed like a bad idea, but at the same time, I remember wanting to go to God with my questions.

Here is the key: there is a significant difference between asking God a question and questioning God's authority.

Has something ever occurred in your life that caused you to question why God allowed it to happen? If you have lived the Christian life for any length of time, it is likely that you have experienced a time when you did not understand what God was doing.

From your limited perspective, His way just did not make sense. Our natural response in difficulty is to ask God, "Why?" Asking God this question with an understanding that He is ultimately in control and that He can do as He pleases means that in the end we trust Him. You can ask God a question without questioning his authority.

But if we question God's authority to allow these circumstances into our lives, there is a greater problem. That is when the seed of pride has taken root, and the idea that we know better than God begins to grow. Ultimately, the end of all your questions should be found in the Word of God, even if that means you don't get an answer to the "Why?"

Trust me, I know that this is hard. I have been there. I hate confusion, and I love solutions. When God doesn't make sense, my mind races with possible scenarios and outcomes. But I am often reminded of a two-word command from the Word of God: *"Be still"* (Psalm 46:10). This is not a pleasant suggestion to rest; it is a command to stop with my control-freak tendencies and know that He is God. He can do whatever He pleases, and I must choose to trust His authority to do so.

So, yes, it is okay to ask God a question, but no, it is not okay to question the authority of God.

Now, I have another question for you: We see that it is never okay to question the authority of God, but is it ever okay to question human authority?

First, there may come a point in which your authority requires that you do something that goes directly against God's Word. In such a situation, Acts 5:29 gives a clear answer: *"We ought to obey God rather than men."* As Christians, we must hold to the Word of God as our ultimate authority, even if that means disobeying a lower authority to do so.

(You should know, however, that being told to clean up your room when you would prefer to go on a youth activity at church is not a conflict between your parents' instructions and God's commands. I'm talking about when an authority tells you to do something that is absolutely, directly opposed to God's Word—like to murder someone or to lie about something.)

Second, there may come a time when something that human authority does goes against Scripture. In such a circumstance, you can do two things:

1. Pray for them. In 1 Timothy 2:1–2, Paul wrote, *"I exhort therefore, that, first of all, supplications, prayers, intercessions, and giving of thanks, be made for all men; For kings, and for all that are in authority; that we may lead a quiet and peaceable life in all godliness and honesty."*

As we saw in Chapter 1, God knows who is in authority and He has allowed them to be there. If they live in ways that are contrary to Scripture, He will deal with them in His time. You must continue to live in a way that follows the Word of God, and trust God to take care of the situation.

It may be that God will lead you to—in the right spirit at the right time—take another step.

2. Speak with them. The Bible gives clear direction on how to speak to someone who has done something that goes against the principles of the Scripture. In Matthew 18:15–17 Jesus said, *"Moreover if thy brother shall trespass against thee, go and tell him* *his fault between thee and him alone: if he shall hear thee, thou hast gained thy brother. But if he will not hear thee, then take with thee one or two more, that in the mouth of two or three witnesses every word may be established. And if he neglect to hear them, tell it unto the church: but if he neglect to hear the church, let him be unto thee as an heathen man and a publican."*

If you sense that you should speak to an authority about something he is doing that is against Scripture, you must pray for God's wisdom and follow His leading.

In many cases, it may be that once you talk to your authority, you find that there was simply a misunderstanding. Or perhaps, when you bring the problem before that authority, he realizes that he is wrong and makes it right before the Lord and with you. In any case, the Bible is clear on how to deal with such a situation, and you are to follow those biblical guidelines. You have no right to talk disrespectfully to or about your authority, especially when you haven't spoken to them or prayed for them.

If an authority figure in your life has made a mistake (and all of us do) but has since made it right, you are to forgive him as God has forgiven you. Ephesians 4:32 says, *"And be ye kind one to another, tenderhearted, forgiving one another, even as God for Christ's sake hath forgiven you."*

Any authority figure whom God has placed in your life who is a Christian is not only your authority, but also your brother or sister in Christ. Galatians 6:1 instructs, *"Brethren, if a man be overtaken in a fault, ye which are spiritual, restore such an one in the spirit of meekness; considering thyself, lest thou also be tempted."*

Do not hold on to the mistakes of your authorities. Forgive them, and learn from their mistakes.

Rebellion manipulates the circumstances.

"And the woman said unto the serpent, We may eat of the fruit of the trees of the garden: But of the fruit of the tree which is in the midst of the garden, God hath said, Ye shall not eat of it, neither shall ye touch it, lest ye die."

God gave Adam and Eve everything they needed. But, out of a heart of rebellion, Eve twisted God's words.

Genesis 2:16–17, gives us God's exact command: *"And the Lord God commanded the man, saying, Of every tree of the garden thou mayest freely eat: But of the tree of the knowledge of good and evil, thou shalt not eat of it: for in the day that thou eatest thereof thou shalt surely die."*

But when Eve talked to the serpent, she added a phrase as she related the command: *"God hath said, Ye shall not eat of it, neither shall ye touch it, lest ye die."*

God had never said that Adam and Eve could not touch it, but by adding those words, Eve made it clear that she believed God's command was unjust. Rebellion of the heart had convinced Eve that God was withholding something from her. Because of this rebellion, Eve misrepresented God.

Earlier I shared that the purpose of authority is to protect you. Satan wants to do everything he can to remove you from a place of protection. Remember his sole goal on earth is to turn men away from God.

If he can manipulate you into rebelling against your authority, he succeeds in getting you to go against God. One of the simplest ways for Satan to get you to rebel against your authority is to convince you that they are withholding something good from you.

Too often teenagers believe the lie that their authorities are trying to keep them from having any fun. Satan wants to blind you to the dangers that lie outside of the boundaries (or, as in our previous chapter, the shark cage) in your life. He doesn't want you to know that crossing the lines will bring you closer to pain and regret. He doesn't want you to see the broken lives of those who went against their authority. He doesn't want you to see the devastating effects of disobedience.

You may think that breaking a rule here and there will never lead to extreme circumstances. That is exactly what Satan wants you to believe. He knows that rebellion is developed one step at a time, and he patiently awaits your demise.

Could I warn you? Don't think yourself so strong that you will not give in to his tricks.

First Corinthians 10:12 admonishes, *"Wherefore let him that thinketh he standeth take heed lest he fall."*

The lie that persuades you into thinking that your authorities want to keep you from enjoying life is the same lie that will convince you that the commands of the Bible are given to make life boring and miserable. If your thinking has been influenced by this lie, you need to rewire your brain by reading the Word of God.

In Scripture, you will find promise after promise of blessing given to those who submit their wills to God and to the authorities He has placed in their lives. Jeremiah 29:11 says, *"For I know the thoughts that I think toward you, saith the Lord, thoughts of peace, and not of evil, to give you an expected end."* Psalm 119:2 says, *"Blessed are they that keep his testimonies, and that seek him with the whole heart."* Psalm 37:4 says, *"Delight thyself also in the Lord; and he shall give thee the desires of thine heart."*

God wants to bless you. He wants you to live a life of peace. But this only comes when you obey the commands of the Scripture and yield your will to God. All his promises are true! Claim them and prove God.

Blessed is that man that maketh the LORD his trust, and respecteth not the proud, nor such as turn aside to lies. Many, O LORD my God, are thy wonderful works which thou hast done, and thy thoughts which are to us-ward: they cannot be reckoned up in order unto thee: if I would declare and speak of them, they are more than can be numbered.—PSALM 40:4–5

Rebellion Denies Truth and Believes Lies

"And the serpent said unto the woman, Ye shall not surely die:"

To tell Eve that she would not die if she ate of the fruit was a blatant lie, yet it was so cleverly disguised by Satan that Eve believed it.

The death God had promised for disobedience was not a physical one. Satan knew that. The death that God warned Adam about was a spiritual death—a separation between God and man that would continue from generation to generation. *"Wherefore, as by one man sin entered into the world, and death by sin; and so death passed upon all men, for that all have sinned"* (Romans 5:12).

Satan deceived Eve into believing the ultimate lie, and he continues to convince men to believe many other lies. One of the lies that Satan uses in the lives of teenagers is the lie that all authority is out to get them. I have heard many teenagers say it. They think their youth pastors hate them. They think that their parents are only trying to make their lives miserable. They think their teachers are attempting to take all the joy out of their lives. Lies, lies, lies!

Satan wants to do everything he can to separate you from your authority because he knows they desire nothing more than to help you and lead you in a right way. Satan doesn't want you to be helped or led in the right way, so he convinces you that you are only being reprimanded because everyone hates you!

You and I both know that no authority figure is perfect. Additionally, I am fairly certain that those in authority in your life do not hate you. In fact, the reason they are constantly after you is because they love you! Remember, they are commanded by God to watch for your soul.

Proverbs 19:18 says, *"Chasten thy son while there is hope, and let not thy soul spare for his crying."* God did not give this command to authority to make you miserable. He did it for your protection. When your authorities correct you, they are not only obeying the command of God, but they are also reflecting the love of God.

Hebrews 12:6 says, *"For whom the Lord loveth he chasteneth, and scourgeth every son whom he receiveth."* Verse 11 continues, *"Now no chastening for the present seemeth to be joyous, but grievous: nevertheless afterward it yieldeth the peaceable fruit of righteousness unto them which are exercised thereby."*

As I write this chapter, my daughter Leighton is fifteen months old. She is just beginning to walk which has only accelerated her spirit of exploration. For whatever reasons, the objects that intrigue her the most are the same objects that can cause her the most harm. Without my wife's and my intervention, Leighton would spend her days playing with wall outlets, eating decorative plants, and placing her small hands in the fireplace. Fortunately for Leighton, her parents love her enough to stop her before the moment of pain. Why do we stop her? To keep her from having fun? No! To make life miserable for her? Of course not! We stop her to protect her.

The authorities in your life have more wisdom than you even know to recognize. They have gone through their teenage years, and, whether or not you believe it, they do know what will cause pain in your life. When they set boundaries and correct you for crossing them, it's not because they want to make your life miserable. They are trying to protect you.

Do not be deceived as to whom the enemy is in your life. The enemy is Satan, not your authority. Second Corinthians 10:3–6 says, *"For though we walk in the flesh, we do not war after the flesh: (For the weapons of our warfare are not carnal, but mighty through God to the pulling down of strong holds;) Casting down imaginations, and every high thing that exalteth itself against the knowledge of God, and bringing into captivity every thought to the obedience of Christ; And having in a readiness to revenge all disobedience, when your obedience is fulfilled."*

When Satan feeds you the lie that your authority is "out to get you," cast down that thought. Remember that the authority figures in your life love you and want what is best for you. Look to the Word of God for truth, and you will find it!

Rebellion Promotes Individual Agendas

"...in the day ye eat thereof, then your eyes shall be opened, and ye shall be as gods, knowing good and evil."

When God told Adam and Eve that they could not eat of the fruit of the tree, He did so for their protection. When Satan persuaded Eve to rebel against God and eat of the fruit, he was doing it for his own wicked agenda.

Satan's goal is to turn men away from God by causing men to question the authority of God and encouraging men to rebel against God. He deceives men into believing that God is withholding something good from them. He convinces men that they are their own god; then, ultimately, he uses those men to bring about the fall of others.

Oh, yes, Satan is crafty, and his ways are covert. He makes rebellion look appealing. He knows that there is pleasure in sin for a season, so he diverts man's attention from the eternal to the temporal. He does all this for himself! You are simply a means to his ideal end. He opposes God, and everything he does stems from that opposition.

Rebellion in man mimics the rebellion of Satan. Rebellion is selfish and seeks to promote its own agenda. Men who have turned away from God only seek to turn others away with them. Paul warns Christians of such men in Philippians 3:18–19 saying, *"For many walk, of whom I have told you often, and now tell you even weeping, that they are enemies of the cross of Christ: Whose end is destruction, whose God is their belly, and whose glory is in their shame, who mind earthly things."* Proverbs 17:11 says, *"An evil man seeketh only rebellion: therefore a cruel messenger shall be sent against him."*

With this in mind, you must determine not only to watch out for the traps of Satan, but also to choose your friendships wisely. Have you ever noticed at a teen camp or youth conference how quickly the rebellious kids from the different youth groups find each other? It usually only takes about a day or two—sometimes just an hour or two! These are the types of teenagers who tend to sit in the very back and complain about how lame the program is, how weird their youth pastors are, and how self-righteous the other teens can be. As individuals, rebelling seems pointless; but as a group, they find consolation in knowing they are not alone. These friendships that are formed, however, are comprised of selfish individuals who want to wallow in their misery. They are not looking out for each other but for themselves.

"Be not deceived: evil communications corrupt good manners" (1 Corinthians 15:33). If you associate with rebellious friends, you will become rebellious. Because rebellion promotes the individual's agenda, these "friendships" are empty and meaningless. Nothing good comes from a friendship founded on

rebellion. Proverbs 13:20 says, *"He that walketh with wise men shall be wise: but a companion of fools shall be destroyed."*

The end of all rebellion is destruction. Those who rebel against authority and choose their own way will eventually reap the consequences. Proverbs 14:12 says, *"There is a way which seemeth right unto a man, but the end thereof are the ways of death."*

Satan, despite all attempts to oppose God and despite his partial success in turning some men away from God, will meet his end. Revelation 20:10 tells of his doom: *"And the devil that deceived them was cast into the lake of fire and brimstone, where the beast and the false prophet are, and shall be tormented day and night for ever and ever."*

Rebellion Removes God's Blessing

"Therefore the Lord God sent him forth from the garden of Eden, to till the ground from whence he was taken" (Genesis 3:23).

The Garden of Eden was a place of protection—a place where all of Adam and Eve's needs were met. When they sinned against God, they were removed from that perfect place of protection and punished for their rebellion. God was no longer a friend to enjoy, but became someone to fear and avoid. The results of rebellion will always be the same. Rebellion will remove God's blessings from your life.

Unlike Satan, God seeks to save men from a harrowing fate. When Adam and Eve sinned, He had a plan to save men from eternal death and restore their fellowship with Himself once again. *"The Lord is not slack concerning his promise, as some men count slackness; but is longsuffering to us-ward, not willing that any should perish, but that all should come to repentance"* (2 Peter 3:9).

God wants to give you a life filled with peace and joy and love. God wants to bless you abundantly! But His blessings can only be found by submitting to His will. The moment that we go against God's will to pursue our own desires, the moment that we rebel against His plan, is the moment we remove ourselves from a place of blessing.

Many blessings come from a right relationship with authority. When you follow your authority's counsel and obey your authority's instruction, you begin to see those blessings. You will begin to gain your authority's trust, and with that trust comes more freedom. With that freedom comes responsibility, but that responsibility is not something to be feared. Responsibility is a part of maturing as a young adult. Trust, freedom, and responsibility are all blessings that come from submission. If you rebel against authority, however, you lose trust and gain more restrictions. Those restrictions are for your protection; but if you continue to rebel, you will break out of those restrictions and place yourself in danger. In that place you will also have responsibilities, but all too often they are responsibilities that an immature and rebellious young person is not ready to bear.

Another blessing that comes from a right relationship with authority is friendship. It will not be the same kind of friendship you experience with your peers, but it is a friendship that encourages growth and is truly enjoyable. When you are submissive and obedient, there is no need to fear your authorities or avoid them. You can learn from your authorities, enjoy their company, and seek their counsel.

As you develop a relationship with your authorities, you begin to understand God's purposes for placing them in your life. Listen to their counsel, honor them, respect them, and pray for them. It's all to your advantage!

> *I exhort therefore, that, first of all, supplications, prayers, intercessions, and giving of thanks, be made for all men; For kings, and for all that are in authority; that we may lead a quiet and peaceable life in all godliness and honesty.*
> —1 TIMOTHY 2:1–2

CHAPTER THREE

Choices and Their Results

Your Response to Authority

When it comes to responding to authority, everyone makes a choice. There is no middle ground.

You will either submit to God and the authority He has established in your life, or you will rebel. Remember, your choice for one is your choice for all. You can't choose to respond to one authority favorably, rebel against another authority, and still claim God's blessings for obeying the one. If you choose to undermine any single authority in your life, you rebel against God.

There are two characters in the Bible that illustrate the contrast between a life of submission and a life of rebellion. Both men were chosen by God to rule as king over Israel. Both men sinned, and both men were confronted by a spiritual leader about their sin. But each man had entirely different responses. In their responses we see the results of rebellion and submission.

You've perhaps guessed the identity of the two men—Saul and David. Let's examine their responses and apply the results to our lives.

Rebellion

The life of Saul is marked by continual rebellion. In 1 Samuel 10, God gave instructions to Saul through Samuel. Saul was to go down to Gilgal and wait for Samuel to offer the sacrifice, and then the Lord would show Saul what to do next.

In 1 Samuel 13, Saul responded to Samuel's instructions in disobedience. Ultimately, he disobeyed God when he offered the burnt offering himself rather than waiting for Samuel. When Samuel confronted him, Saul explained and excused himself, revealing not only his disobedience but his failure to trust in the Lord. Samuel responded, *"Thou hast done foolishly: thou hast not kept the commandment of the LORD thy God, which he commanded thee: for now would the LORD have established thy kingdom upon Israel forever. But now thy kingdom shall not continue: the LORD hath sought him a man after his own heart, and the LORD hath commanded him to be captain over his people, because thou hast not kept that which the LORD commanded thee"*(1 Samuel 13:13–14).

Saul continued to make foolish decisions, following his own whims rather than seeking the Lord's guidance. His rebellion reached its climax when the Lord commanded Saul to utterly destroy Amalek, sparing nothing. Instead, Saul spared the life of the king as well as the best of the spoils, including animals. Once again, Samuel confronted him, and once again, Saul explained and made excuses. This time, he blamed the people and claimed that the animals were saved to give to the Lord as an offering. Samuel responded with a judgment from God: *"And Samuel said, Hath the* Lord *as great delight in burnt offerings and sacrifices, as in obeying the voice of the* Lord*? Behold, to obey is better than sacrifice, and to hearken than the fat of rams. For rebellion is as the sin of witchcraft, and stubbornness is as iniquity and idolatry. Because thou hast rejected the word of the* Lord*, he hath also rejected thee from being king"* (1 Samuel 15:22–23).

Because of Saul's choice to rebel against Samuel, and ultimately against God, God removed the blessings that He wanted to give Saul. First Samuel 28:15–18 gives us a tragic glimpse of one of Saul's last moments before he died. In great distress because the Lord would not answer him and because he feared the Philistines, Saul went to a witch in an attempt to discover the outcome of the next day's military battle. In an apparent act of God that surprised even the witch, Samuel (who had since died) appeared and delivered a final indictment, a judgment from God, to a still-rebellious Saul:

> *And Samuel said to Saul, Why hast thou disquieted me, to bring me up? And Saul*

answered, I am sore distressed; for the Philistines make war against me, and God is departed from me, and answereth me no more, neither by prophets, nor by dreams: therefore I have called thee, that thou mayest make known unto me what I shall do. Then said Samuel, Wherefore then dost thou ask of me, seeing the LORD is departed from thee, and is become thine enemy? And the LORD hath done to him, as he spake by me: for the LORD hath rent the kingdom out of thine hand, and given it to thy neighbour, even to David: Because thou obeyedst not the voice of the LORD, nor executedst his fierce wrath upon Amalek, therefore hath the LORD done this thing unto thee this day.—1 SAMUEL 28:15–18

Saul's life shows us that rebellion is a result of pride. Rebellion disregards God's commandments and elevates selfish wants and desires. It may bring temporary satisfaction, but rebellion always leads to tragedy.

Rebellion will move a young person from a place of safety and blessing to a place of danger and disaster. Decide now that you will submit to the authority that God has given you. For an example of that submission, notice the life of David.

Submission

In contrast to Saul, David's life is marked by consistent submission to God. This does not mean that David was perfect—he wasn't. Nor does it mean that he never disobeyed God—he did. The difference was in his heart toward God. While Saul's heart was full of pride and willfulness, David's was tender and responsive.

David's submission is perhaps most clearly seen in his humble response when confronted by a spiritual authority with his sin. Second Samuel 12 records how David confessed his sin in humility and sought after righteousness.

As you may know, David had taken another man's wife for himself, and she became pregnant. In an attempt to cover his sin, David had the woman's noble husband killed and then hastily married her to remove any questions that could have arisen concerning her pregnancy.

The Lord sent the prophet Nathan to point out David's sin. David broke in humble repentance: *"And David said unto Nathan, I have sinned against the LORD. And Nathan said unto David, The LORD also hath put away thy sin; thou shalt not die. Howbeit, because by this deed thou hast given great occasion to the enemies of the LORD to blaspheme, the child also that is born unto thee shall surely die"* (2 Samuel 12:13–14).

David's sin was not without consequences. However, because he willingly listened to the message of the Lord and confessed his sin, David continued to be blessed by God for the remainder of his life. First Kings 2:2–4 records some of David's final words spoken to his son Solomon:

> *I go the way of all the earth: be thou strong therefore, and shew thyself a man; And keep the charge of the LORD thy God, to walk in his ways, to keep his statutes, and his commandments, and his judgments, and his*

testimonies, as it is written in the law of Moses,
that thou mayest prosper in all that thou doest,
and whithersoever thou turnest thyself: That
the Lord *may continue his word which he*
spake concerning me, saying, If thy children
take heed to their way, to walk before me in
truth with all their heart and with all their
soul, there shall not fail thee (said he) a man
on the throne of Israel.

Submission to God and to the authority He establishes will always result in blessing. It does not mean that things will be perfect, but it does mean that you can claim the promises of God and trust that He will work everything out according to His perfect plan.

When it comes to responding to authority, you must make a choice. Looking beyond today to the outcomes of your options, there is really only one sensible choice—faith-filled submission.

Trust in the Lord *with all thine heart; and*
lean not unto thine own understanding. In all
thy ways acknowledge him, and he shall direct
thy paths.—Proverbs 3:5–6

CONCLUSION

Time, Proof, and Blessings

If you're much like me, I suspect that as you were reading the introduction to this little book, you felt compelled to inform me that it is no longer a hard, fast rule on all airlines to turn your cell phone off. Indeed, as of this writing, some airlines do now allow the use of cell phones in the air.

But it wasn't always that way—and I had plenty of mental arguments with flight attendants in the interim!

As cell phones became popular, no one knew for certain how they would affect the aircraft's communications and navigation equipment. Because of such uncertainty, it was safer to ban the use of cell phones than to risk the loss of lives through their use.

The only way to prove whether or not cell phones were dangerous on airplanes was time. (That, and asking me. But the Federal Communications Committee, the FCC, doesn't ordinarily ask me for my opinions!) So time passed, engineers conducted studies, and, in the end, I was right. But truth be told, although my opinions were strong, there was no way I could have actually known whether the use of my cell phone was safe or not. I am not an avionics specialist; I simply had an opinion.

I suspect that in several more years, cell phone use will be allowed on all planes during takeoff and landing, proof that even the "experts" can be wrong.

When it comes to the principles of God's Word, however, there is no error. What was wrong in the Garden of Eden is wrong today. What was right for the first-century Roman Christians is right today. God's Word is perfect and unchanging.

Human authorities (including the FCC) make mistakes. You may have authority figures who set particular boundaries simply because they do not know what the outcome will be. They may believe it is safer to make a rule and let time reveal the truth than it is to let you run free and end up hurt in some way. Trust them. They have lived longer than you and have experienced more than you. In the end, it may be that you are right, but let God reveal that in His time.

When you submit to God-given authority, you demonstrate trust in God. And when you trust God, you can rest in His promise of safety and blessing.

> *But it is good for me to draw near to God: I have put my trust in the Lord GOD, that I may declare all thy works.*—PSALM 73:28

Visit us online

strivingtogether.com

wcbc.edu